PLATFORM PAPERS

**QUARTERLY ESSAYS ON THE PERFORMING ARTS
FROM CURRENCY HOUSE**

**No. 58
February 2018**

CURRENCY HOUSE

Platform Papers Partners

We acknowledge with gratitude our Partners in continuing support of Platform Papers and its mission to widen understanding of performing arts practice and encourage change when it is needed:

Neil Armfield, AO
Anita Luca Belgiorno-Nettis Foundation
Jane Bridge
Katharine Brisbane, AM
Elizabeth Butcher, AM
Penny Chapman
Dr Peter Cooke, AM
Sally Crawford
Wesley Enoch
Ferrier Hodgson
Larry Galbraith
Wayne Harrison, AM
Campbell Hudson
Lindy Hume
Professors Bruce King and Denise Bradley, AC
Justice François Kunc
Dr Richard Letts, AM

Peter Lowry, OAM and Carolyn Lowry, OAM
David Marr
Helen O'Neil
Lesley Power
Professor William Purcell
Queensland Performing Arts Centre Trust
Geoffrey Rush, AC
Dr Merilyn Sleigh
Maisy Stapleton
Augusta Supple
Christopher Tooher
Caroline Verge
Queensland Performing Arts Trust
Rachel Ward, AM and Bryan Brown, AM
Kim Williams, AM
Professor Di Yerbury, AM

And we welcome our
MAJOR CORPORATE
SPONSOR FOR 2018

To them and to all subscribers and Friends of Currency House we extend our grateful thanks.

Platform Papers
Readers' Forum

Readers' responses to our previous essays are posted on our website. Contributions to the conversation (250 to 2000 words) may be emailed to info@currencyhouse. org.au. The Editor welcomes opinion and criticism in the interest of healthy debate but reserves the right to monitor where necessary.

Platform Papers, quarterly essays on the performing arts, is published every February, May, August and November and is available through bookshops, by subscription and online in paper or electronic version. For details see our website at www.currencyhouse.org.au.

THE CHANGING LANDSCAPE OF AUSTRALIAN DOCUMENTARY

||||||||||||||||||||||||||||||||||||||||||||||||||||||||||||||||||||||||||||||||||||||

TOM ZUBRYCKI

ABOUT THE AUTHOR

TOM ZUBRYCKI is the eldest son of a Polish immigrant family who settled in Canberra in 1955. After completing a Bachelor of Science at the ANU he moved to Sydney where he worked as a science and maths teacher before enrolling for a master's degree in sociology at the University of NSW. By the early 1970s Zubrycki was a leading participant in the video access movement, before starting on his first film, *Waterloo* (1981), a historical account of a battle by residents against the redevelopment of their inner Sydney suburb. This was soon followed by *Kemira, Diary of a Strike* (1984) and *Friends and Enemies* (1986). In the 1990s he turned his attention to migrant and refugee stories. *Billal* (1995) traced the impact on the life of a Lebanese-Australian family disrupted by a racially motivated attack. *Homelands* (1992) told the story of a refugee family torn apart by their conflicting desires for a new life or a return to their homeland.

In 1996, after a short break as commissioning editor at SBS, Zubrycki returned to filmmaking. His documentaries included the highly regarded *The Diplomat* (2000), a profile of freedom fighter Jose Ramos Horta in the final turbulent year of his campaign to secure independence for East Timor, and *Molly and Mobarak* (2003) a story exploring the friendship between an Afghan asylum-seeker and a young woman in a country town. His more recent work includes *The Hungry Tide* (2011) and *Hope Road* (2017). Between making his own films, Zubrycki continues to mentor and produce the work of early-career writer/directors, many of them Indigenous. These documentaries include *Stolen Generations* (2000), *Gulpilil: One Red Blood* (2002), *The Panther Within* (2006), *Mad Morro* (2009) and *Teach a Man to Fish* (2018).

Over 40 years he has produced and/or directed more than 36 documentaries, several of which have received awards or nominations. They include AACTAs for Best Documentary (*Kemira, Diary of a Strike* and *The Diplomat*) and an International Emmy for *Exile in Sarajevo*. His films have screened at festivals around the world. In 2009 Zubrycki was presented with the Cecil Holmes Award for his ongoing career support for directors. A year later he received the Stanley Hawes Award in recognition of his outstanding contribution to documentary filmmaking in Australia. He has served on the editorial board of *Filmnews*, the boards of the Australian Directors Guild, the Australian Screen Directors Authorship Collecting Society Ltd (ASDACS), Metro Screen, the program committee of the Australian Documentary Forum (OzDox) and is on the Sydney Film Festival film advisory panel. For six years he taught documentary at the University of Technology, Sydney, and now teaches occasional masterclasses in documentary at the Australian Film, Television and Radio School. His website is www.tomzubrycki.com

Acknowledgements

I would like to thank the many colleagues who shared with me, in the process of writing this paper, their thoughts and concerns about the precarious state of Australia's documentary sector. I am especially grateful for the responses and opinions of fellow documentary makers Martha Ansara, Lizzette Atkins, Rebecca Barry, Anna Broinowski, Margie Bryant, Sharon Connolly, Michael Cordell, Pat Fiske, Mitzi Goldman, Sam Griffin, Madeleine Hetherton, John Hughes, Simon Nasht, Paige Livingstone, Ivan O'Mahoney, Jeni McMahon, Andrew Pike, Catherine Scott and Randall Wood.

Documentary is a vast subject to write about, and I simply didn't have space to address the educational sector, which was part of what used to be called the 'long tail' of broadcast documentary. It remains so, but now it's very much a sector in itself, with web videos, classroom teaching resources, corporate programs, instagram direct action videos, art gallery installations and so on. Nor did I have space to consider virtual reality documentaries, which have quickly evolved to occupy an important creative niche in the non-fiction space.

Thanks to Katharine Brisbane, Sandra Alexander and Nick Herd for inviting and encouraging me to write this paper, and for their subsequent constructive feedback throughout the process. I would like also to acknowledge the generous assistance given to me by the Screen Australia Strategic Policy and Industry Insight Unit.

Thanks also to the Motion Picture Distributors Association of Australia, the Australian Directors Guild and the Screen Producers Association.

I am immensely grateful to my friends Warwick Pearse, Les McLaren, Peter Kennedy and Rob Pullen for their generous support through the last months of writing. I thank especially my partner Julia Overton, who was of enormous help in re-reading drafts and sharing her insights with me, not only as a filmmaker, but from her years of industry experience at the AFC, the FFC and Screen Australia. Without the help and encouragement of Julia and our son Sam, I doubt whether I could have finished this paper.

Introduction

*A country without documentary films is like
a family without a photo album.*—Patricio
Guzmán, Chilean documentary filmmaker

Documentaries matter now more than ever.
Documentary storytelling is a vital way to explore, and
make sense of, our world and of who we are as a nation; it
is essential to a healthy and democratic society. It allows
us to walk in another's shoes, to reflect the life, hopes,
dreams of ordinary people, to build a sense of shared
humanity, to give voice to the marginalised, and to
strive to hold those in power to account. Documentary
is about telling stories that matter

It's a form of storytelling that doesn't have any rules
as such. Stories can be told in different ways, using
various styles and techniques. They are portraits of real
people, using real life as their raw material constructed
by the filmmaker who makes myriad decisions about
what stories to tell and to whom, and for what purpose.
Documentaries can be poetic, they can be an observed
slice of life or they can be distinctly issue-based. They
are as much an art form, as *about* real life and that's
sufficient reason for them to have a strong cultural
imperative.

In the evolving digital era, a new documentary landscape has emerged in Australia and around the world. Much has changed: greater access to storytelling tools, an expanding client base—but with reduced government funding, new philanthropic involvement and increased fragmentation of the distribution sector.

Over the past decade the old TV broadcast industry has re-structured itself markedly around ratings and perceived audience taste. Where once there was diversity in form and content, there's been a narrowing. Single documentaries on television mostly have been replaced by presenter-driven series and factual reality programs which, once seen as intrusive, are now standard prime-time viewing.

It is outside the broadcast sector that we must look for ambition and innovation. Most documentary film-makers no longer rely on traditional sources of funding but instead are branching out on their own—seeking support from philanthropic foundations, pitching to online platforms like YouTube, crowdfunding, or simply self-funding. Yet despite the digital era presenting new opportunities, most of us working in the sector are facing a grim and uncertain future. Fashioning a career from making documentaries has never been easy, and as one colleague commented: 'We are awaiting the new dawn, it's not there yet.'

But there's hope of change on the way. Netflix and Amazon Prime are entering the Australian industry. They should be made to fund local content, as has already been the case in Europe and Canada. The clamour for regulation of these streaming platforms in the name of the Make it Australian campaign is well under way.

Looking back over my life I can trace my passion for documentary back to the 1960s. We lived in Canberra at the time, and my father often took me to Sydney when he had meetings, and would drop me at the State Theatre while he was away on business. This art deco palace was used exclusively for stage productions, but downstairs there was a theatrette, which showed newsreels. Here I remained, riveted to the screen watching Menzies and Doc Evatt strut the political stage, the drama of the Redex Rally, and quirky suburban stories. Little did I realise that I was watching history in the making; or that two decades later my first documentary, *Waterloo* would screen in the main theatre upstairs and take out top prize in the Greater Union Awards at the 1981 Sydney Film Festival.

Over the course of 37 years I have made my reputation and livelihood from producing and directing documentaries. I've always been inspired to tell stories about ordinary Australians—stories that have been sidestepped by the mainstream media. Mostly they've been single stories that tell a complete narrative, feature unique characters and have a point of view. It's been an extraordinary privilege to do so, and to be able to access government funds. Privileges, however, always come with costs attached. Documentary making is demanding work, seldom well paid, and negotiating subject matter is often personally and ethically challenging.

At the outset, I should say that it's impossible to be passionate about the films you make and not be passionate about the industry you work in, and to continually want to improve it, to make it fairer and better, and ensure that we documentary filmmakers are not the poor cousins of the drama sector in both TV and feature. I hope that it's in this spirit that people will respond to the thoughts and issues I raise in this paper.

1. Early years of documentary

It was a horse race: the 1896 Melbourne Cup, which is generally credited as the first documentary made in Australia, though it was essentially nothing more than a silent recording of an event. In the same year the Lumière brothers arrived in Australia and opened a picture theatre in Sydney known as the Salon Lumière. The Salon's first local offering was that very first recording of a Melbourne Cup.

Commercial operators like the Lumières immediately grasped the potential of movies as entertainment; but it took a few years for government to appreciate the medium's potential. During the months of preparation for the 1901 Federation celebrations, no one in the NSW Government thought to record the ceremony until the very last minute. At that time every available camera in Australia was owned by the Limelight Department of the Salvation Army based in Melbourne. The Army had formed a company as early as 1892 to harness the potential of lanternslides to communicate their message; and quickly grasped the utility and power of film. Small docudramas were combined with slides and gramophone records in their lecture presentations.

As the new form of entertainment gained in popularity, local cameramen, working on their own or hired by entrepreneurs, began shooting, processing and then projecting short reels of film: news items and 'scenics'. From 1909, they became regular weekly newsreels, known as gazettes, which brought together several news items into one ten-minute reel.

These 'cameramen were not just taking pictures, they were multi-skilled filmmakers', wrote Martha Ansara in her book *The Shadowcatchers*, 'because right through the silent period they were not in a position to specialise in cinematography alone.'[1] The newsreels they shot and directed were the primary means by which Australians were able to see their own country and people on screen.

When the talkies took over from silent films, the audience for cinema expanded, and newsreel companies Cinesound and Movietone quickly flourished in Australia and recruited cinematographers to exploit this opportunity. Among them was Frank Hurley who moved into cinematography from still photography. Frank ran a thriving picture postcard business, and became a showman, director, producer and adventurer. He travelled to the Antarctic with Douglas Mawson on several of his expeditions, filming *Home of the Blizzard* (1913); and later, with Ernest Shackleton. The photography of Shackleton's sinking ship being slowly shattered by the pack ice contributed to his fame.

Following the outbreak of World War Two the Government exploited the worth of wartime movie propaganda. What became known as the Films Division was inaugurated within the Department of Information, News and Information Bureau. Cinematographers were recruited to shoot and direct documentaries about campaigns that involved Australian diggers. One of the cinematographers commissioned was Damien Parer, whose documentary *Kokoda Front Line!*, made through Cinesound, captured a respectful portrayal of Australian soldiers and their native bearers during the New Guinea campaign. It was the first Australian film to win an Academy Award.

After the war, there was a further expansion of 'documentary' filmmaking, albeit of an educational nature. Government-driven filmmaking really got into its stride. The Australian National Film Board (ANFB) was set up in 1945, influenced partly by the visit of the Scots filmmaker John Grierson. Grierson was credited with starting the British documentary movement, where he'd inaugurated a system of state-sponsored non-fiction film. He transferred the British model to Canada in 1939 and then proposed a similar model for Australia. Grierson had a strong belief that film could be enlisted to build social cohesion and national consensus.

When the ANFB started to recruit directors and producers to make documentaries along Griersonian lines, not all the newsreel cameramen were impressed.

I came back from the war ... We plonked our cameras and tripods down and we're getting introduced to blokes: 'He's a producer and he's a director', and we'd never laid eyes on these buggers in the 15, 20 years beforehand [...] we were all technicians, and they were all documentary.[2]

While government documentary was taking off, the early optimism of the immediate post-war years motivated a group of cinephiles to produce their own documentaries. The Realist Film Unit was established in 1945 with a commitment to expose pressing social issues, and this led to commissions by the Brotherhood of St Laurence. Among these short documentaries was *Beautiful Melbourne* about the desperate state of those living in slum housing.[3]

In 1949 the Dutch filmmaker Joris Ivens visited Australia as film commissioner for the Netherlands East Indies government in exile, and quickly became aware of his government's opposition to the anti-colonial liberation movement emerging in the region. Ivens resigned his appointed post and embarked on making the landmark *Indonesia Calling*. This 22-minute documentary depicts seamen and dockworkers refusing to service the Dutch ships carrying arms and ammunition destined for Indonesia to suppress the country's independence movement.

Ivens intended the film to create an impact, so despite the Australian Government's attempts to censor screenings, *Indonesia Calling* was widely shown. But the Cold War (1947–53) security environment was such that Australian intelligence soon took an interest in those involved with the making of it. Several of the local artists and filmmakers who helped Ivens ended up being blacklisted.

In 1956 the ANFB changed its name to the Commonwealth Film Unit (CFU), which through the 1950s and 60s became the focus of government documentary production. A lot of the films were promotional, while others were educational. Arguably the CFU's finest achievement of that era was Ian Dunlop's *Desert People* and his *People of the Western Desert* series (1966-70) in which he took two Aboriginal families from a government settlement back to their country where they showed him aspects of their life in the desert. This series was widely shown within Australia and internationally and was greeted with much acclaim. Australia has had a proud tradition of ethnographic filmmaking going right back to A.C. Haddon's Cambridge University expedition to the Torres Straits in 1898, which gave us the first moving image record of Torres Strait Islanders.

In the 1950s filmmakers had to exercise considerable initiative to make their own films, and they could only manage to do it if they got commercial backing. John Heyer was one such individual. Heyer left the Films Division to run the Shell Film Unit where he was asked to produce a documentary that would associate this Anglo-Dutch company with Australia. The result was *The Back of Beyond*, which celebrated the life of an outback postman bringing mail to country towns and stations. It quickly became a popular (and later a critically celebrated) film, seen by 750,000 cinemagoers—though a big proportion of the audience were reportedly given tickets by Shell. A nice bit of promotion work!

Meanwhile back at the Commonwealth Film Unit a 'stable' of in-house directors was selling Australia to the nation and the world.

These films of the post-war boom were films of construction, of prosperity and progress. Sometimes explicitly, sometimes implicitly expressing the nature of the new nation to be built. Every large company and every government instrumentality, and even some of the more militant trade unions, it seemed, felt the need to instruct, exhibit and celebrate on film.[4]

No union exemplifies this more than the Waterside Workers' Federation, which formed its own Film Unit in 1953. Over the next five years the members of the unit—Jock Levy, Keith Gow and Norma Disher—working collectively, produced 21 films on subjects like pensions for veterans, the housing shortage and industrial relations—all from the unionists' viewpoint. A Kombi van doubled as a production vehicle and a screening platform. Screenings took place during lunchtimes at work sites, in union halls and in private homes. As often as possible the unit made good use of wharfies playing themselves in re-constructed scenes. Some of these films, such as *The Hungry Mile*, became documentary classics.

The dawn of Independent documentary

In 1969, Liberal Prime Minister John Gorton established the Experimental Film and TV Fund, which six years later was re-branded as the Australian Film Commission (AFC). After two decades of drought, interrupted by the brief appearance of the experimental filmmaking collective Ubu Films, suddenly nothing was impossible either in content or style.

The Australian Film Commission's development of documentary in the 70s no longer needed the seal of approval, the mark of Menzies-era conformity, from Canberra's public servants.[5]

Government supplied the funds but, with the introduction of peer assessment, no longer had control over the films they supported. Initially, drama features and shorts were funded; the first documentary was Richard Brennan's *Or Forever Hold Your Peace*, about the 1970s moratorium against the Vietnam War.

However, production couldn't happen in a vacuum. The next question was how to get these films to audiences. This is how the Filmmakers Co-op came into existence. As a result of many meetings, and over meals at the O'Fung restaurant in Glebe, it saw its mandate as an exhibition and distribution organisation run by the filmmakers themselves. An operational grant from the Film and TV Fund saw the Sydney Filmmakers Cooperative open its premises in St Peters Lane, Darlinghurst in 1973, followed soon after by co-ops in

Melbourne, Brisbane and Adelaide.

The St Peters Lane office was on the first level, and below was an 80-seat cinema where audiences packed in to watch local and overseas documentaries, short dramas, animation and experimental films. Women were especially active in the co-op, and many films by women about women, funded through the newly formed Creative Development Branch of the AFC, were made and shown. These included Martha Ansara's *Film For Discussion*, Sarah Gibson's and Susan Lambert's *Size Ten*, Jeni Thornley's *Maidens*, and Helen Grace's *Serious Undertakings*. They had a ready audience and a social change agenda, as John Hughes notes:

> *Identity politics enabled the co-ops, as distribution and marketing enterprises, to create new products for newly created markets, and this in turn transformed the institutions themselves, and their cultural practice. The filmmakers' co-operatives were hubs; they articulated 'the movement' in their cultural form and practice, at the same time as they distributed and exhibited the moving image production that performed the zeitgeist.*[6]

Inside the Commonwealth Film Unit the winds of change were also blowing. Younger filmmakers shared ideas inspired by broader social change and aesthetic innovations of the British 'free cinema' movement of the late 1950s, followed on by *cinema verité* in France and the US-born 'direct cinema'. They struggled against the conformism that had become institutionalised, and personified for many in the figure of the CFU's CEO Stanley Hawes. The films that stood out included *Stirring* by Jane Oehr—about high-school students and corporal punishment, and *The Man Who Can't Stop* by Mike Rubbo, which followed his uncle's efforts to stop sewage being pumped into the ocean rather than recycled to farmland.

Similar new trends were emerging within the ABC. In the late 1960s, the Commission's internal production unit took the lead in developing series like *A Big Country* (1968–91) and *Chequerboard* (1969–75) which examined aspects of Australian life so far avoided: divorce, mental illness, gay rights and migration. Disappointingly, *Chequerboard* was short-lived; the ABC returned to caution, announced with the arrival of the bland presenter-driven shows, as in *Bill Peach's Australia* (1975–76).

As generous film funding became available through the support of the Creative Development Branch, increasingly directors who had been trained and employed by the ABC left the organisation to set up their own production companies. Directors such as Bob Connolly, Robin Anderson, Nick Torrens, Aviva Ziegler and Curtis Levy launched successful careers as independents.

While the majority of early independents made films on 16mm, others, like myself, began experimenting in half-inch reel-to-reel portapak video. In 1974 these early and rather primitive recording machines became available through video-access shopfronts funded through a Whitlam Government initiative based on a similar Canadian scheme called Challenge for Change. In theory anyone could walk off the street and be trained in how to use this technology. What made it exciting was that people could shoot video and replay it straightaway without the costly laboratory procedures of 16mm technology.

I was one of those filmmakers who exploited these new opportunities. In 1974 I borrowed a camera to film a Balmain residents' street-corner protest over an incident involving a large container truck that had crushed a small car and killed two nurses inside. A colleague taught me the rudiments of editing and then I screened the finished documentary, ironically titled *You Have to Live with it,* to a crowded Balmain Town Hall. Later an updated version was shown in private to the state transport minister. The trucks were eventually banned from the area.

I spent the next three years making issue-focused videos, in conjunction with local community groups. For many of us this was where our filmmaking careers started. Most of us switched to 16mm because video technology was still so crude. However film required a budget, and a budget was dependent on AFC funding. This funding, however, never demanded compromise, even when the subject matter was politically sensitive. We saw ourselves as determinedly *independent* filmmakers, and that label set us apart from directors working inside government bodies like Film Australia and the ABC.

This discourse was often highly individualistic, celebrating as it did the auteur, and hostile towards received authority and 'conformism'; it practised an editorial militancy that challenged journalistic dedication to 'objectivity' and 'balance'.[7]

Landmark documentaries from that period included Martha Ansara and Essie Coffey's *My Survival as an Aboriginal*, one of the first documentaries in which an Indigenous Australian was directly involved in deciding how she and her community would be represented. Gil Scrine's *Home on the Range* gave an insight into the US base at Pine Gap; *Angels of War*, directed by Andrew Pike, Hank Nelson and Gavan Daws, showed the villagers' perspective on the PNG World War Two campaigns; and Pat Fiske's *Rocking the Foundations,* followed the story of the NSW Builders Labourers Federation. Other documentaries pushed new boundaries: *Two Laws,* by Alessandro Cavadini and Carolyn Strachan, was made with the Booroloola community and the Aboriginal subjects were also collaborators.

By the mid-1970s the filmmakers' co-ops were the established centres of the independent filmmaking community. Between 1975 and 1985 the Sydney Co-op had a staff of up to seven people processing their grow-ing collection of films. These were rented by schools, TAFE, universities, libraries and film societies. People continued to crowd the cinema—there was no other opportunity for the public to see these Australian-made films, certainly not on television. When the Sydney Co-op closed its doors it had 325 titles in its catalogue and 90 in active distribution. Most of these titles were documentaries.

Meanwhile the ABC was still making documentaries in-house, and it took the corporation some time to think more deeply about sourcing its Australian documentary programs from 'outside'. Independent documentary filmmakers—individually and collectively—argued strenuously for this to happen. We could, after all, prove demand from audiences in the cinema, and we could not understand why our films were not getting to the small screen. Paddington Town Hall was the favourite location of many protest meetings. I recall the outrage when we heard that David Bradbury's Academy Award-nominated film *Frontline* (1979) had been sold to the BBC but rejected by the ABC. 'There were two separate worlds.' Mark Hamlyn remembers:

> *It was kind of like the Cold War. There were those who lived inside the ABC and then there were those who swarmed around the AFC and were in the Film Co-op ... It's a great tragedy but there it is.*[8]

The ABC eventually began to purchase our documentaries, but their choice was haphazard at best. It was the Australian Film Commission that became the catalyst for change. In 1984 it inaugurated a documentary fellowship scheme with the ABC. Filmmakers fortunate enough to obtain fellowships could make a film on a subject of their own choice, and I was lucky enough to be amongst the first recipients.

Amongst the fellowship films were: Dennis O'Rourke's much debated *Good Woman of Bangkok*, about the day-to-day life of a Thai prostitute and her relationship with the filmmaker; Susan Lambert and Sarah Gibson's experimental film *Landslides*; and John Hughes' *All That Is Solid*, a speculative documentary taking the future of Australia as its subject. My fellowship film, *Friends and Enemies*, was a documentary about the vicious and long-running Queensland power workers' strike of 1985. Others included Bob Connolly and Robin Anderson's *Joe Leahy's Neighbours*, which traced the fortunes of Joe Leahy, the son of a gold prospector and explorer who lived amongst a tribe in the PNG highlands; and Gary Kildea's *Celso and Cora*.

2. 10BA and the era of the Accords

In 1984, on the occasion of the award of the first AFC fellowships, executive producer Tom Haydon famously branded most documentaries as 'garbage', and the majority of those making documentaries as 'filmmaking illiterates', accusing their work of being 'stale, bland and uncaring'.[9]

Tom Haydon's comments in the context of the notorious 10BA (1981–89) were understandable. 10BA was a tax concessions scheme introduced by the Hawke Government, which allowed a 150 per cent tax concession on their investment at risk. The larger the budget, the greater was the potential tax write-off to investors. Yet there was no in-built requirement for distribution. Six hundred documentaries were made between 1981 and 1989, of which a great proportion received little distribution.

When the tax benefits for private investors were reduced significantly in 1987, a series of government reviews of film and television resulted in the establishment of the Film Finance Corporation (FFC) in 1988. It was to be the Government's principal agency for funding film and television production, and documentaries were to have an important place in the new agency. Meanwhile the AFC was targeted with the cultural remit to encourage and develop practitioners, innovation, research and marketing

Of the overall FFC funding, documentaries were scheduled to receive only five to 15 per cent in a given year, and needed a demonstrated 'market interest' to trigger immediate support from the new agency. But it was enough for the ABC to recognise at last that this outsourcing was a far more cost-effective way of getting documentaries made than by in-house production—especially when they had to provide only 25 per cent of the budget, and the FFC the rest.

The ABC's first documentary unit for outsourced production was established under Jonathan Holmes' leadership in 1987. That same year the very first Documentary Conference (later known as the AIDC) was held in a winery in McLaren Vale, South Australia. I was one of 130 delegates. The conference had something for everyone. People partied hard and much wine was consumed between discussions around craft issues and screenings of recently completed local documentaries.

It was at the 1987 conference that Holmes announced he had secured a dedicated budget of $2 million to pre-purchase independent work for the ABC. Before long the pre-sale arrangements between the FFC and broadcasters were formalised into what became known as the Accords: the ABC would agree to pre-purchase 20 documentaries within a single financial year, starting in 1992–93. Successful projects had to fit a rationale of 'cultural relevance' to Australian audiences. Among the early Accord documentaries were Pat Fiske's *For All the World to See*, about the eye surgeon Fred Hollows; Carol Ruff and Ned Lander's *50 Years of Silence*, the story of Carol's mother, Jan Ruff-O'Herne, and her experience of enforced prostitution during World War Two at the hands of the Japanese military; and Ruth Cullen's *The Tightrope Dancer*, an exuberant portrait of the eccentric dancer and artist Vali Myers.

SBS was soon to follow with seven-to-ten documentaries a year, after the Keating Government launched its major cultural policy initiative *Creative Nation* in 1994. Under this initiative SBS established a commissioning wing for outsourced production—SBS Independent (SBSI). My documentary *Homelands,* about an El Salvadorian refugee couple, and the tensions within their marriage, was one of the first documentaries that received a pre-sale under this scheme.

For documentary filmmakers the Accords were a boon. They provided a much-needed measure of predictability, including a guaranteed minimum number of commissions to compete for; and a continued capacity to initiate a one-off project, especially one of specific interest to an Australian audience. This gave the filmmaker and the industry a significant degree of stability. It had reached critical mass.

The FFC, however, took a slightly different view. Two years into the Accords, it was evident that they were not recouping well. The Accord documentaries were of limited interest to international broadcasters or sales agents. Accordingly, the FFC moved to create a non-Accord category. Non-Accords must secure an overseas pre-sale or distribution guarantee to trigger support. It didn't take long before Non-Accords began to attract an increasing share of FFC funds at the expense of Accords. Susan Mackinnon, FFC documentary investment manager, led a concerted effort to create and broker links between producers and key broadcasters, sales agents and distributors in Europe and North America. This process continued under her successor, Julia Overton.

The 1990s became the heyday of independent documentary production. In one year alone (1994–95), the ABC released 62 hours of first-release Australian documentaries in prime time—20 were FFC Accords, ten non-Accords, ten Film Australia and 22 acquisitions. SBS broadcast 66 hours of local material. There was no doubt that the Accords had brought independently produced Australian stories to ever-increasing audiences. This had never happened before to this extent. But there was a catch. Most Accord titles had been made for Australian television, without further distribution to cinema or festivals. Feature-length documentaries designed for cinema were becoming a rarity. Theatrical exhibition of documentary had slumped from 20 in 1988 to six in 1992.

The Australian Film Commission stepped up to fill the space by creating the Special Production Fund to support programs that had no marketplace attachments. This tended to favour more edgy and non-commercial programs which were funded with festival and cinema release in mind. One of them was Lawrence Johnston's *Eternity*—the story of Arthur Stace, the man who for decades wandered the streets of Sydney, writing in perfect copperplate the word 'Eternity' on the pavement in yellow chalk. *Jade Babe,* by Janet Merewether, was a genre-bending documentary about the everyday issues faced by a very tall woman who worked as a dominatrix. Another was *Exile in Sarajevo,* which I produced, and for which the director, Tahir Cambis, travelled to Sarajevo at the high point of the Balkans war. Gothic in feel and texture, the documentary exploited the graininess of early video cameras to the limit. Yet another, innovative both in form and content, was *One-way Street,* John Hughes' evocation of the legacy of Walter Benjamin.

Towards sustainability

An ever-pressing issue for filmmakers has been how to create an industry capable of making a living for those who work in it. In 1992, after three years of Accords, the FFC still appeared to have done little to support or help create a viable infrastructure for documentary makers. FFC support came in the form of an investment. How did they expect us to survive from film to film, we asked, when 80 cents of every dollar the film earned went back to the government? Revenue from Screenrights, the non-profit collection agency, was a cause of particular frustration. Screenrights was set up specifically to administer the funds collected when educational institutions copied programs broadcast on television. These were usually the largest source of returns for a local film and were crucial to keeping our companies afloat and growing our business. Calls by filmmakers to have greater equity in their films were by now sounding loud and clear. The producers were being represented by the Screen Producers Association (SPAA) and the directors by the Australian Screen Directors Association (ASDA). The ASDA Documentary sub-committee was the most active and contained both directors and independent producers—who were often one and the same person. The sub-committee had been functioning since 1987, and we took turns convening it. The committee became an important policy forum taking complaints to the broadcasters. And there was certainly no shortage. The ABC's publicity department came within our sights as a target, for not promoting programs sufficiently through media outlets. Overseas buy-ins were getting preferential treatment, Trevor Graham noted. Why, for instance, were home-grown documentaries being delegated to the Thursday 9.30pm timeslot, while overseas documentaries were running at prime time? Wasn't this cultural cringe?[10]

Having a strong industry voice was becoming increasingly important. The industry successfully lobbied for a quota to be imposed on each commercial television licensee, requiring them to broadcast ten hours of first-run 'social issue' documentary. But when the legislation went through Parliament in 1998, it contained no requirement for the commercial broadcasters to source any of their content from independent producers. Most of the programs ended up being made in-house. Pay television was also exempt from these requirements and remains so.

In 1996 the Keating Government, which had been a great supporter of the arts, lost at the ballot box. The Liberals were back in power, and the Howard Government wasted no time in appointing David Gonski to review federal government assistance to the film industry, and to determine 'the extent of any unnecessary overlap or duplication between the Commonwealth's support mechanisms'.

When the Gonski Report was released the following year, the industry was relieved that the status quo had largely been preserved. Gonski argued for the 'funding envelope' to be maintained 'in the medium term', and that the 'many doors' funding policy should remain. (Documentary makers had always argued that they needed a variety of doors through which they could apply for funding.) The report's only controversial recommendation related to Film Australia, which depended on the allocation of an annual grant, entitled the National Interest Program (NIP). Film Australia had a mandate under the NIP to 'produce programs that deal with matters of national interest to Australia and the Australian people'. Many notable documentaries had been made there over the years including Graham Chase's *Thirst*, a no-holds-barred look at the trauma of living with an alcoholic; Mark Lewis's *Cane Toads*, a

satirical 'horror' documentary about Australia's infesta-
tion of cane toads; and Trevor Graham's *Mabo—Life
of an Island Man*, a film on the life of the land rights
campaigner Eddie Koiki Mabo.

Gonski's recommendation was that Film Australia's
Lindfield site be sold-off, and the organisation become
a commissioning body instead of a producing body.
This sparked opposition from the Film Australia board;
and the Government rejected both proposals. Richard
Alston, the responsible federal minister, described the
organisation as 'the jewel in the documentary crown'.[11]

The next ten years under CEO Sharon Connolly's
leadership were a watershed. At a time when the non-
Accord sector was expanding, and focusing on attracting
pre-sales from international broadcasters, Film Australia
became a haven for experienced filmmakers to tell
Australian stories to Australians. These included *Rats in
the Ranks*, Bob Connolly and Robin Anderson's acute
observational commentary on the electoral machina-
tions of the Leichhardt Council in Sydney; *Cunnamulla*,
Dennis O'Rourke's controversial portrayal of life in
a western Queensland town; and my own film, *The
Diplomat*, about Jose Ramos Horta and the final year
of his campaign for an independent East Timor.

As the 1990s wore on, SBS's commissioning started
to increase. SBSI, under the leadership of Bridget Ikin,
and later Glenys Rowe, built a strong culture of commissioning independent work with a diversity of style and
content. Authored works were encouraged, including
Gill Leahy's *Our Park*, which examined the conflict

between local interest groups over a rare piece of urban bush, and followed the developing action over twelve months. There were other memorable documentaries including Peter Hegedus' *Inheritance: A Fisherman Story* and *Grandfathers and Revolutionaries,* which drew on his Australian-Hungarian roots.

SBS Independent also created opportunities for Indigenous filmmakers like Darlene Johnson, who wrote and directed *Stolen Generations,* about the government-initiated removal of children from Aboriginal families, and Rachel Perkins, who together with Bec Cole and Darren Dale made the ground-breaking series *The First Australians: The Untold Story of Australia* (2008). This seven-episode series chronicles the history of contemporary Australia from the perspective of its first people. Perkins, along with Warwick Thornton, Erica Glynn, Bec Cole, Mitch Torres and Allan Collin, started out as Indigenous trainees at Central Australian Media Association (CAAMA) Productions. CAAMA was established in 1988 to service Imparja Television, a remote-area commercial broadcast service based in Alice Springs. It continues to this day to train and support Indigenous producers and directors, and has close ties with local Aboriginal communities. CAAMA's successful documentary series, *Nganampa Anwernekenhe,* showcasing the diversity of life in Central Australia, now comprises over 200 short documentaries produced over thirty years.

Independent documentary in the late 1990s was buoyant. ABC's Arts commissioning was strong, with

Curtis Levy's *Hephzibah*, the story of the celebrated concert pianist and human rights worker Hephzibah Menuhin; and Daryl Delloro and Sue Maslin's *The Edge of the Possible* about Jörn Utzon and the design and construction of the Sydney Opera House. Meanwhile on SBS, Storyline Australia had become the weekly slot for one-off Australian documentaries. It was highly popular, achieving audiences up to 547,000 for a single documentary. The films varied stylistically and in terms of content and presentation. They included: *A Wedding in Ramallah* by Sherine Salama, an intimate observational documentary set in the West Bank about a young Palestinian couple; *Painting with Light in a Dark World*, by Sascha Ettinger Epstein, about a Kings Cross photographer documenting Sydney's inner-city street life; and my own film *Molly and Mobarak*, about the relationship between a Hazara asylum seeker and a teacher in a NSW country town.

Prior to their television premiere many of these documentaries also played at film festivals and in cinemas. In the early 2000s it was possible to see a local or overseas documentary at the movies almost once a week. In Sydney alone there were three cinemas that screened independent films: the Valhalla, the Mandolin and the Chauvel. But as video stores started to proliferate, the heyday of independent cinemas came to an end.

3. The rise of the series

With the closure of independent cinemas came major changes in the documentary sector. Television commissions for one-off documentaries were becoming rarer. Series, and especially formats, were becoming more popular with networks. The language was changing as well. The word 'factual' started replacing 'documentary'. As John Hughes noted:

> *Australian documentary production in recent years has been configured from a practice of independent filmmakers developing and producing work in an artisanal mode, like novelists, writers, independent scholars or painters, in favour of a rationalized 'creative economy' where consolidated larger companies deliver factual programming as outsourced producers to television broadcasters.*[12]

This thrust into consolidation was seen by the funding bodies as a good thing to create sustainable businesses following the British model, but received strong opposition from independent solo filmmakers, including myself. At a presentation to AIDC in 2006 in my role as ASDA's documentary representative, I argued that, 'We have no problem with large companies but their encouragement and support should not be at the expense of the rest of the documentary sector [...] The future is not moving out of the back office, it's making the back office more viable.'

Our arguments fell on deaf ears, and, as broadcasters gave increasing preference to limited types of documentary series, docu-soaps, reality-based and factual programming, it was also becoming clear that the 'golden age' for single documentary was indeed over. An AFC discussion paper summed it up:

> *The emphasis on light-factual series and reality-based observational formats has seen the traditional stand-alone social or essay documentary become a relatively endangered species. This has implications both for the diversity and level of sophistication of content in Australian documentaries, as well as the level of documentary skill of Australian practitioners.*[13]

The documentary culture had changed dramatically, and almost overnight. Top-down commissioning from the broadcasters now largely dictated content, and was based on perceived audience taste. Twenty years earlier it was the interests and passions of the filmmakers that had driven the content.

As a response to this rather gloomy analysis, the FFC in 2005 set up the Special Documentary Fund to assist more distinctive risk-taking work that did not require a market attachment. Among the films funded were

Amiel Curtin-Wilson's *Bastardy*, about the celebrated actor Jack Charles and the dark side of his criminal 'career'; and Juliet Lamont's *The Snowman*, about her father Jimmy's descent into schizophrenia after several years of working in Antarctica. Some genre bending documentaries even managed to access the FFC's Feature Fund. One was Anna Broinowski's ground-breaking *Forbidden Lies,* a hybrid documentary that investigates the enigma of a best-selling book purporting to be a non-fiction story of the honour killing of a young Jordanian woman by her family.

Nothing was to illustrate the decline in one-offs more dramatically than the axing of Storyline Australia by SBS program executives. Since 2001 Storyline Australia had provided a regular slot for documentaries. It had held its own and had achieved consistently high rat-ings. However, figures in 2007 revealed that audiences that year had varied considerably—sometimes low, sometimes high, and ratings varying from 60,000 to 470,000 viewers per episode. It was not the stable audi-ence that management wanted, and they had something else up their sleeve. Soon the mystery was revealed. SBS had acquired the British format *Top Gear* and made a commitment of $11 million to the production of a local version. Most of us in the independent documentary sector were incensed that precious commissioning funds were being diverted to this series.

But this was just the beginning. The focus of TV commissioning had definitively moved to entertainment and ratings. Formatted content already had a proven record, especially in the UK, with programs like *Who Do You Think You Are?* and SBS was to keenly embrace the trend, and acquire licensing rights to make similar series in Australia. Reality programming was also on the rise. Reality TV-style 'documentary' was nothing new in Australia. It had started back in 1992 with *Sylvania Waters*. Billed as a 'real-life' soap opera, this twelve-part co-production by the ABC and BBC followed the lives of a family who had allowed a live-in camera crew to film virtually 'anywhere, at any time'. *Sylvania Waters* was the start of a whole spate of factual reality programming that 'observed' the experiences of carefully selected casts in purpose-built settings, which usually incorporated an element of competition.

Sylvania Waters was a franchise, as were most of the other series that began to dominate Australian factual TV: *Big Brother Australia* (2001–08) for Channel 9 was one of the most publicised and high-rating formats of this type. Others included *The Colony* and *Outback House*.

Australia also had some home-grown formats of its own. In 2006 *Bondi Rescue* was commissioned from Hilton Cordell by Channel 10, and in 2019 is still running, now owned and produced by Cordell Jigsaw Zapruder (CJZ). The program, about the working days of lifeguards patrolling Sydney's Bondi Beach, has been on-sold to over a hundred international territories.

These formats and reality shows were immediately taken up by the networks because they were relatively cheap to make and equally cheap to commission, with minimally staged events, amateur casts and the use of lightweight digital cameras. These shows averaged ratings double those for single documentaries, and they attracted a new, younger audience to non-fiction programming.

Reality programming caused a split in the documentary community. For some directors it provided useful employment, while others frowned on these new formats. The criticism was that they led to a dumbing down of television, pushing 'true' documentary to slots later and later in the evening. These trends were already evident but, as it turned out, instead of being the death knell of documentary, the form would fast re-generate itself. But not without some interim pain.

Government reshapes the industry

In May 2007, a press release by Senator George Brandis, then Minister for the Arts and Sport, heralded major changes. Brandis announced the formation of a new agency, the function of which was 'to help develop a high quality commercially focused Australian screen production industry'. The new agency was to be an amalgam of the FFC, AFC and Film Australia.

Documentary makers were alarmed, and through the guilds immediately called a number of urgent meetings, in particular to query what implications the Minister's emphasis on 'commercial success' would have for documentary. Not everyone was of like mind. At the initial meeting filmmaker Michael Cordell presented a document which cast into sharp relief the gap between commercial and auteur-driven positions.

Let's kill the silly 'documentary' versus 'factual' argument [...] Let any idea about real people in the real world be based on its merits and relevance, not some arcane idea of what is more 'creative', 'worthy' or 'cultural'. We kill our creativity if the new screen agency ends up dictating what sort of genre we're allowed to make. Let's build the whole sector at this point—not create turf wars between ourselves.[14]

Differences were put to one side as questions suddenly loomed over Film Australia's future. If the new screen agency was to take over administering the NIP, what would become of this venerable organisation, the buildings, the precious library, and the superstructure of executive producers?

Ten years earlier the independent film community had rallied in support of Film Australia, but this was not the case now. For years since the Gonski Report there had been a growing disillusion with the top-heavy executive-producer driven structure. Also, the culture of the organisation had changed.

Back in the 1990s Film Australia was a place where idiosyncratic, and even, on occasion, auteurist documentary voices were nurtured. But in its final years before incorporation into Screen

Australia, more expository and less subjective voices became the norm and its institutional voice was less diverse.[15]

Not everyone agreed with the dismantling of Film Australia. Martha Ansara cautioned, 'not to let a history of personality clashes and opposition to past policies at Film Australia blind us to the potential value of its resources (and even traditions) for Australian society and our hard-won documentary community'. Filmmaker Dennis O'Rourke responded just as passionately, arguing:

It's taken too long to reform the organisation, and from the perspective of many of us, the legal, creative, and commercial relationships between Film Australia and the people who actually make their films remain inadequately inefficient and unfair. We don't want to be pickled in aspic.[16]

But the consensus to do away with the old models had an unstoppable momentum. On 15 August 2007 a letter written to George Brandis signed by 60 of Australia's leading documentary filmmakers called for dramatic changes and for a major revamp to the way the agency's $12 million in annual funding for documentaries was dispersed.

This move heralded the beginning of the end for Film Australia, but we filmmakers didn't get all we wanted. The National Interest Program fund ended up being merged into other funds, and lost its unique identity. Meanwhile the building was put up for sale, and the valuable library moved into the National Film and Sound Archive. The proceeds of the building sale might well have been recycled back into the documentary sector but that was not the decision. When Screen Australia opened for business the funding doors for documentary had shrunk dramatically to two: one fund triggered by television commissions, the other by innovation and intrinsic merit. The latter came to be called the Signature Fund which was eventually merged into the Producer Program and lost its autonomy.

It was hard to grasp just how quickly the ground had moved. The closure of funding doors meant that a small group of executives within the two broadcasters now held extraordinary powers. The ABC and SBS continued to commission programs from independent companies, but increasingly they were the large companies, many underpinned through the Screen Australia Enterprise Scheme. In 2009, under the scheme, $9 million was awarded to 12 production companies. Over time these companies built a cosy output deal with the broadcasters producing series and format television.

There was no holding back on the indignation. At the 2011 AIDC Bob Connolly spoke out loudly and emotionally:

> *Our public broadcasters are transforming our industry—concerned with artistry and high endeavour—into a sausage factory, turning out,*

with some very honorable exceptions, what can only be described as fodder [...] it's like shrinking the national creative gene pool for genetically modified factual television.[17]

In an essay, 'Who Killed Documentary?' published in *The Australian*, Trevor Graham lashed out at factual series.

Why am I whingeing, and what do 'one off' stories provide that series don't? Am I just bitching about change I don't like? It is summed up with one all-important word, DIVERSITY. A top-notch Australian 'one-off' documentary will engage, entertain, inform and educate audiences, and even trigger water cooler discussions next day. They are an important arm of our 'civic culture' [...] and they help put the 'public' into 'public broadcasting' by holding up a mirror to our life as a nation. But the move to factual series radically cuts across these values of diversity. Not only do we now have fewer stories from fewer producers, but the breadth and depth of stories and storytelling is vastly reduced.[18]

In November 2012 at the annual Australian Directors Guild Conference, a group of us launched the Indiedoco Campaign to save the single documentary. At the Conference I argued for a boost to Screen Australia's Signature Fund to salvage the 'one-off'. The fund nurtured a particular culture, a creative freedom not driven by the marketplace. Budgets were small, but resulted in a huge range of films—from Mick Angus's *Salt* about photographer Murray Fredericks and his journeys to Lake Eyre; to Robert Nugent's *Night Parrot Stories*, an exploration of the mythology and science surrounding the elusive nocturnal bird; to Helen Barrow and Hugh Piper's *Dancing with Dictators*, about Australian publisher Ross Dunkley and his battle of the control over the *Myanmar Times*, which was picked up by the BBC.

The campaign quoted from a research study by Sharon Connolly, which showed the average annual hours of non-fiction since 2007–08 increased by 34 per cent on the previous five years to 311 hours, but of that, 76 per cent was documentary series hours and just 24 per cent single documentary.[19]

The domination of the series, and the ratings success of reality television, had its flow-on effects. The directors, who would otherwise have been developing their own projects, ended up getting jobs as directors-for-hire. On these series the director's work was severely circumscribed. Their job was to be on location with the crew, and deliver the rushes. Once delivered, the editors and producers took over. Directors were not allowed in the cutting room. Some directors took personal gambles and refused to work on series; and instead found producers for their own projects and built successful careers. Jen Peedom was one of them. Her feature documentary *Sherpa*, which told the story of the 2014 Mount Everest avalanche from the Sherpas' point of view, was a critical and box office success.

Not all series, however, were 'documentary lite'; some were genuinely original and ended up contributing powerfully to the national debate. *Once Upon a Time in Cabramatta* was a three-part SBS-commissioned series produced by Northern Pictures, about a suburb of south-west Sydney, told from the point of view of the Vietnamese Australians who lived there. It was produced and directed by Bernadine Lim, who became Head of Documentary at Screen Australia in 2018. The series traces the arrival of refugees in the 1970s, progresses to the time when Cabramatta was the heroin capital of Australia, and ends with the suburb standing as a migrant success story. SBS followed this with another series *Once Upon A Time in Punchbowl*—this time a serious look at the Lebanese community and issues of integration.

The ABC's *Changing Minds* was likewise a breakthrough series, in that it was the first time cameras had been allowed inside a mental health unit to follow patients at risk of developing mental illness. The success of the series did, however, paper over the de-prioritising of documentary within the ABC. History and natural history were the casualties. As Kim Dalton pointed out in his May 2017 Platform Paper, 'History should be core to the ABC's remit. It has the responsibility to reflect our own lives back to ourselves in both a contemporary and an historical sense.'[20] Up to 2012–13 the ABC had been commissioning and broadcasting around 15 hours of history documentaries each year, including Peter Butt's *Who Killed Dr Bogle and Mrs Chandler?*, which presented new evidence in the mysterious death of a couple after a New Year's Eve party, unsolved for four decades. But in 2013 history was now no longer a priority, and neither was natural history. This proud unit, which had run for 40 years and was an innovator in the field of nature documentaries such as the award-winning *The Dragons of Galapagos*, was completely dismembered.

Philanthropy to the rescue

By the turn of the millennium documentary had to find new avenues of support. The US had always had a strong philanthropic culture, and some of that money was finding its way into the documentary sector. It was an acknowledgment that documentaries were socially engaged projects capable of outreach and social impact; so it was only a question of time for this same approach to take hold in Australia.

One of the first documentaries to pioneer this approach was Sascha Ettinger Epstein and Ian Darling's *Oasis,* a campaign film aimed at reducing youth homelessness and focusing on a youth refuge in inner-Sydney run by the Salvation Army. *Oasis* screened on the ABC, was followed by a panel discussion and became 'event television'. Various philanthropists also joined an interactive website, which supplied DVDs and press kits.

The Documentary Australia Foundation (DAF) had been launched in 2007 by Darling himself, who was a philanthropist as well as filmmaker. DAF had Tax Deductible Recipient Status, enabling donations from other foundations and individual donors to be steered to particular films. Some of this funding would go into production and some into advocacy and outreach. The private donations could be combined with government agency funding and pre-sales. Mitzi Goldman, CEO of Documentary Australia Foundation, recalls that it was hard in the early days:

> *We certainly struggled [...] There was a lot of scepticism [...] DAF was not going into the space to plug the gaps in the diminishing government funding for documentaries, because the case could not be about just supporting the art form of documentary. For philanthropic support it's really about the issue areas that documentary highlights.*[21]

Goldman decided she needed a documentary to wrap her arms around in a very pro-active way: a distinctive social issue film and one that could serve as a prototype for similar projects. She chose *I Am a Girl*, by Rebecca Barry: a gentle coming-of-age documentary about six girls and what it means to grow up female in the twenty-first century. The film had already been rejected by broadcasters and funding bodies. At the suggestion of a potential funder, Goldman drew up a shortlist of ten films in the funder's areas of interest, which were narrowed down to *I Am a Girl*. They came on board with a development grant.

Meanwhile Barry had run a small but significant crowdfunding campaign, and had had many meetings and conversations with funders to whom Goldman had introduced her. Finally it was at a philanthropic function arranged by Goldman that two funders agreed to commit significant funds to propel the film into production. Barry also secured a sizable grant from her own relationships and contacts. With six key funding and outreach partners committed around the film, *I Am a Girl* was launched and six years on continues to make an impact through outreach and fundraising campaigns. Well over two hundred hosted screenings have been held to support a variety of projects—some local and some overseas.

I Am a Girl became a 'poster child' for DAF. It proved that solid issue-based films could definitely ignite interest from the philanthropic sector. However, it took filmmakers some time to understand the model and exploit the opportunities. The work of finding your own grant-makers was more difficult than at first appeared, and it still remains so. It's not easy to cold-call a potential philanthropist and prick their interest. DAF recognised that it had a lot of work to do to build capacity in the sector. It needed to make a significant investment in time to educate, offer workshops for filmmakers, and even executive produce certain projects.

It was in this context that GOOD PITCH[2] AUSTRALIA came about. GOOD PITCH was already a tried and tested brand. It had originated in the UK as BRITDOC and brought together filmmakers with NGOs, foundations, philanthropists and social entrepreneurs. It became the 'rocket fuel' for DAF. Shark Island Institute and the Documentary Australia Foundation brought the first of three GOOD PITCH[2] AUSTRALIA events to Sydney in October 2014.

The well-chosen audience of 300 at the Sydney Opera House was agog. Filmmaking teams pitched their film and their associated outreach campaign to a room full of philanthropists, key influencers and partners from the not-for-profit sector, advocacy groups, and educators. In total, $2.2 million was steered towards seven projects. In following years GOOD PITCH[2] and GOOD PITCH[3] added $11.8 million, which funded 12 additional social issue documentaries and their impact campaigns.

The list of completed films included Kelrick Martin's *Prison Songs*, a 'musical' about Indigenous incarceration; Sophie Wiesner's *Call Me Dad*, about men and domestic violence; Maya Newell's *Gayby Baby*, about gay families bringing up children; and Damon Gameau's *That Sugar Film*, a documentary warning of the damage done by sugar in society. Screen Australia contributed development funding in some of these cases and it just proves how critically important this aspect of the agency's work continues to be.

Through GOOD PITCH the idea of socially driven feature-length documentaries exploded, and traditional distributors got on board. Madman hired an 'impact producer' and released *That Sugar Film* across Australia. The film developed an enormous fan-base, with social media, Q&A launches, community screenings, a school action toolkit and an app. The impact producer was a new position, which rapidly became a standard item on budgets of documentaries with a social change agenda. Teri Calder, one of the pioneers in this area, describes it as an evolving space:

> *The role requires a diverse skillset. It is part social researcher, social change strategist, part fundraising, distribution and marketing specialist. It involves working creatively with filmmakers and a coalition of aligned partners to identify the goals (the impact you want to create with the film) and the most effective strategies to deliver the film from completion to impact. Then comes the work of making it all happen.*[22]

The success of GOOD PITCH coincided with the rise of crowdfunding platforms, and cinema-on-demand models putting less reliance on distributors and old models of exhibition. Distribution started to be driven by the filmmakers themselves surrounded by people who wanted to use film to make change.

GOOD PITCH has now run its course in Australia, but philanthropy remains a permanent feature of the funding scene. In 2018 Shark Island launched a twelve-month development lab which invested in six projects with a social impact slant per year. Each team selected receives ongoing mentoring and support, including $25,000 in development funding.

Philanthropy is not suitable for every film; not every documentary is overtly issue-based, or has a strong social impact component. A vast number are simply stories that focus on interpersonal relationships, 'buried' histories, or the zeitgeist in general. These documentary genres are incredibly hard to get funding for these days. Broadcaster interest is rare, and screen agency support is now extremely competitive, especially since direct government funding to the sector has fallen significantly in the past five years allowing for inflation.[23] Unlike in previous decades, there is now comparatively little space for documentarians to develop a distinctive voice.

4. Broadcast television features and online

In recent years we have seen a radical shake out in the old television broadcast model. So what place will documentary have in this new factual environment? According to statistics released by Screen Australia, documentary series production rose from 295 hours in 2011–12 to 366 hours in 2016–17. Yet only 21 single-title documentaries were shown on television or cable in 2016–17 compared to 51 five years earlier. This includes commissions and acquisitions.

The two public broadcasters are largely format and series driven; though they still commission a small number of one-offs. SBS annually commissions four single documentaries for the *Untold Australia* series, while ABC commissions some single documentaries preferring that they play across multiple platforms. *True Crimes Stories* is a recent example. Budget cutbacks, especially at the ABC, play a bigger part in commissioning considerations than ever before. Also it's cheaper for ABC and SBS to market a series than an individual program. Rating requirements dominate broadcast decisions, even more so now that online has severely cut into TV audiences. How many times have we been told, 'You have an excellent program but it's too *niche* for us. We're only interested in subjects that have broad public appeal.'

Eventually many (but, unfortunately not all) of the documentaries funded through the various state and federal agencies are purchased by the broadcasters, once they are presented to them as acquisitions. But when they do make a purchase, it is at a fraction of the cost of commissioning them. This was the case with *The Namatjira Project*, the iconic story of the Namatjira family, tracing their quest to regain the copyright of their grandfather's artwork. The film was originally turned down by the ABC, but when it was broadcast by the network in 2017 it achieved excellent ratings, and audiences gave it a score of nine out of ten on internal measures of quality and distinctiveness.

With these results it's a shame that the ABC doesn't commission more one-off's, rather than waiting and then acquiring them at bargain price on completion. Although Steve Bibb, Head of Factual, seems to leave the door open:

> From my commissioning point of view, I don't have a specific policy in relation to series and one-offs for Factual [...] To me, it's always about the strength of the story. [...] Creativity, storytelling, form and what's best for the audience should lead.[24]

Where once there existed a whole range of small independents whose business plan relied on a broadcast commission every one or two years, now there are few—and fewer still who work in the area of co-production. One exception is Simon Nasht of Smith & Nasht. His latest feature as executive producer is a one-hour science documentary, *The Kingdom of Fungi*, directed by Annamaria Talas. Fungi, the world's largest and oldest of organisms, was a subject with genuinely universal appeal.

Nasht wanted to fund the film as an official co-production with CBC in Canada and for that he needed an Australian broadcast partner. The ABC declined a pre-sale. Eventually National Geographic (Australia) consented, which triggered the 'pathway to (local) audience' required by Screen Australia's Offset Department. Then European and North American distributors signed up and Nasht was able to start production. A year later the program had been sold to more than twenty countries and won several major awards. According to Nasht, himself a producer of 25 years' experience: 'It's never been tougher because the domestic market is so thin.'

Chris Hilton, CEO of Essential Media, and one of Australia's most prolific producer/directors, likewise struggled to fund his series *Living Universe,* which examines the quest to find extra-terrestrial life by 'the brightest minds in space exploration'. The documentary, a combination of a four-part series and a feature documentary, is allegedly the most expensive ever made out of Australia and took six years to finance and produce. *Living Universe* did get a licence fee from the ABC, but at a reduced rate. Marketplace attachments that flowed into the budget were: distribution guarantees against various territories, presales from North American streaming sites and European broadcasters, grants from Screen Australia, Create NSW, the Offset and investment from a post-production house. The 90-minute version played at Event Cinemas and very quickly afterwards the series appeared on the ABC.

The Kingdom of Fungi and *Living Universe* are complex and expensive projects to finance out of Australia, mainly because national broadcasters have a remit to commission Australian stories. This gives them a perfect reason to say 'no'. However, they do not shy away from re-makes of foreign formats that have been developed and road-tested overseas.

While Kim Dalton was Head of Television at the ABC TV (2006–13), the broadcaster had a blanket ban placed on foreign formats. This is no longer the case. SBS never had that reservation. In the 2017–18 financial year, Screen Australia funded five factual series based on formats developed overseas, including *Filthy Rich and Homeless, Teenage Boss* and *War on Waste 2*. The agency contributed $2.66 million to these series: 17 per cent of the total Documentary Department budget. This has caused considerable alarm. On 25 May 2018, 37 producers, concerned at the impact this was having on the local independent sector, put their names to a submission pressing Screen Australia to refuse to finance such productions.

Every foreign format produced means that a local production opportunity has been lost. Local ideas create Australian owned IP—giving future income potential to local companies and investors—[and] raise the expertise in the local talent pool in program development. Locally developed shows help sustain an economically viable independent production sector.[25]

Getting behind original Australian formats is to me a 'no brainer'. It makes sense for screen agencies to assist in the development of new formats, and the idea of a 'format lab' is gaining in popularity. Anything to quell the tide of overseas formats dominating our small screens and devices.

The producers' submission also raised alarm about BBC Studios, a new Australian production arm of the BBC opening its doors in Sydney. The company will be eligible to apply for Screen Australia funding despite being the operator of five TV channels in Australia broadcast on Foxtel. One of the quirks of the broadcasting regulatory landscape is that instead of the channel itself holding the broadcasting licence, Pay TV carriers are the licensees of all the channels they carry. The letter demanded that the BBC Studios loophole be closed immediately:

The relaxation of funding restrictions, together with reduced funding and consolidation of foreign ownership of the local industry, is increasing competition for ever-diminishing Screen Australia production investment. The few remaining Australian-owned companies must now compete in the domestic market against extremely well-resourced, vertically integrated multi-nationals, which are receiving public funds designed to encourage Australian culture.[26]

Responding to the producers' submission Michael Brealey, Chief Operating Officer of Screen Australia, responded. 'Screen Australia sees value in not limiting which projects can receive its funding, provided at all times they will be made as Australian stories of relevance and interest to local audiences.'[27]

Screen Australia's response has stunned the sector. It has always been assumed that industry programs are meant solely to support Australian cultural producers, but apparently this is no longer the case.

The rise of cinematic features

Today there is a growing public demand to experience documentaries on the big screen. This is the case the world over. Cinematic documentary is booming. In the US there's talk of a 'golden age'.[28] Here in Australia, where there's also been a striking resurgence of documentaries in the cinema, the trend is similar. Between 2007 and 2011 only 38 documentaries achieved cinema release. In 2017, in just one year, a total of 19 Australian documentaries were released. These included *Mountain* by director Jennifer Peedom; *The Namatjira Project* by

Sera Davis and Sophia Marinos; and *The Opposition,* a David-and-Goliath battle over land in Papua New Guinea by director Hollie Fifer.

Jimmy Barnes: Working Class Boy was one of the most successful of the 18 released in 2018. Produced by Michael Cordell of CJZ and distributed by Universal, *Jimmy Barnes* ran up $823,000 on 230 screens—the widest release to date for an Australian feature documentary. After a few weeks' theatrical run, the film turned up on Channel Seven, securing an audience of 1.2 million. According to Cordell, 'the approximately 40,000 who saw the film on the big screen certainly did not affect the ratings'.

Releasing *Jimmy Barnes* just prior to television showing was a smart move because the film piggy-backed off the publicity generated by Barnes himself in the mainstream media and which spilt over into the broadcast. This kind of marketing is something that ABC and SBS have traditionally resisted, determined instead to keep the premiere run for programs they commission, but in so doing depriving themselves of festival showings and theatrical runs. In my opinion this 'first window' requirement is short-sighted because it denies the producer the opportunity of building the film's profile.

Jimmy Barnes is at one end of the scale. At the other end in the marketplace are a whole lot of low-budget features, many of which garner as much attention as (and sometimes more than) the bigger budget ones. In October 2018 *Backtrack Boys,* directed by Catherine

Scott, a character-driven film about youth at risk in rural Australia, opened on 60 screens, helped in no small way by a social-impact producer and off the back of a successful film festival run at which it had achieved a lot of awards and publicity. *Backtrack Boys* deployed the new 'alternative content cinema' platform, which means a film has a typical run of only a limited number of screenings a week at a single cinema, and thereafter has the chance of building up an audience from week to week.

The ways these two documentaries were financed, however, were quite distinct. *Jimmy Barnes* was a sizeable Channel Seven presale. Screen Australia funds and the Offset covered the remainder. *Backtrack Boys* was initially self-funded; then DAF got behind it as executive producer and finally they secured funding via Screen Australia's Producer Program.[29]

The Producer Program has four rounds per year and on average receives 18 applications per round, most of them feature films. In 2017–18 only eight features were funded, approximately 15 per cent of the submissions. The investment managers concede they turn down very good applications. I believe that this all-or-nothing approach needs a fundamental re-think, one that acknowledges the organic, evolving nature of documentary production. At the 2017 AIDC Sam Griffin called for such a new approach and proposed what she called the Progressive Fund. She underpinned the philosophy of the fund in her MSAB thesis:

In documentary filmmaking, particularly creative documentary making, the lines between the development, pre-production, production and post stages are blurred; they intersect and inform each other, often in non-sequential ways that can't always be predicted in scripts and treatments.[30]

Griffin suggests that funding be distributed progressively over multiple stages, with subsequent funding depending on a continuing positive trajectory of the project. Each project would be given a series of smaller grants, rather than a single large one. She envisages four stages with up to fifty projects per year receiving seed funding, of which 25 would get through to the second stage, ten to stage three, and eight to stage four. 'In this model the agency spreads its exposure to risk across a greater number of projects at an earlier stage, allowing both unknown filmmakers and/or unpredictable stories a chance to test ideas.'[31]

What would happen to projects that don't make the cut after having received some funding? Griffin suggests they could be finished in other ways—perhaps self-fund at first and later apply to Screen Australia's Producer Equity Program (PEP);[32] or they could attract interest from distributors, broadcasters or philanthropists. This model involves calculated risks, but Griffin argues that in her model only the very best receive funding through to completion. In the end, she claims, the payoff will far exceed the risk and result in broadening the pool of voices in Australian documentary filmmaking and the types of films produced. Isn't this what screen agencies are mandated to do?

Filmmaker Anna Broinowski, on the other hand, believes that while Griffin's new model could provide invaluable opportunities for emerging filmmakers and projects, Screen Australia also needs to do more to support high-end feature documentaries for theatrical and digital platforms.

> *Australian feature documentaries consistently punch above their weight at film festivals around the world, and have held their own against Australian dramas, both at the local box office and on new cinema-on-demand and SVOD platforms: from Jen Peedom's* Mountain *which grossed $2.13 million, to* That Sugar Film *(1.71 million) to Taryn Brumfitt's* Embrace *($1.13 million), to Kitty Green's audacious Netflix hit,* Casting Jon Benet. *With contemporary filmmakers blurring the fact/fiction boundary for increasingly genre-agnostic audiences, the doco/drama divide in film financing is outmoded. Feature documentary makers with cinematically ambitious, international projects need the same upfront creative and financial surety as drama filmmakers working with similar budgets.*[33]

Making a feature documentary can often be a long, hard road. It can take years if it follows an unpredictable narrative, and I wonder how many promising films are started but never finished? How many important opportunities are missed, to share with audiences new and different stories about Australia and Australians?

Online documentary

Opportunities are evolving for original short-form content on new online platforms, but not as fast as filmmakers would like; and the licence fees paid, with few exceptions, are quite small.

Screen Australia is crucially involved in many of these initiatives. One has been with *The Guardian* newspaper, which in 2018 commissioned four local documentaries for YouTube, and another with Vice. In 2014 Screen Australia launched a joint initiative with Google called 'Skip Ahead'. To be eligible for funding, a 'content creator' needed an existing subscriber base of at least 25,000 on YouTube. Science communicator Vanessa Hill was one of the successful applicants. Her channel boasted 450,000 subscribers. Hill then approached Margie Bryant of Serendipity Productions, who succeeded in getting sizeable presales from YouTube for two of Hill's projects: *Mutant Menu*, an immersive look into genetic engineering, and *Attention Wars*. Both were supported by the Screen Australia initiative. 'Online works to its best advantage when it's short-form', Bryant observes. 'A one-hour long form usually needs to be re-written as a short-form series.'[34]

In August 2017 *The Australian* newspaper premiered a new project: *The Queen and Zak Grieve*, a six-part documentary investigation by Ivan O'Mahoney and Nial Fulton. The six ten-minute films told the story of Grieve, a young Indigenous man convicted of murder and facing a life in prison under Northern Territory's mandatory sentencing laws. The series was launched on *The Weekend Australian*'s website in daily instalments. In the same way that many of the great (audio) podcast shows have unexpected twists and turns, O'Mahoney notes, 'We wanted this series to have unexpected moments as well. We wanted to keep the viewers guessing.'[35] Foxtel acquired the rights to a 90-minute version of the project. For them a tie-in with another Newscorp entity was enticing.

ABC Documentaries had been commissioning occasional series for their iview platform, but it was ABC Indigenous that took a risk with *Black As*, a 24-part sharp and funny adventure series of five-minute episodes, set in Arnhem Land. It confounded the commissioning editor Sally Riley's expectations, getting over a million views. ABC Arts funds four different series, each made up of six five-minute programs called Artbites, also for iview, and aimed at emerging filmmakers. Artbites is supported by Screen Australia and is in its third year.

SBS, too, has been an innovator in this new space. In August 2018, the network launched a world-first, live documentary for Instagram called *She Called Me Red*— the personal journey of Yunus, a 27-year-old Rohingya man now living in Melbourne. Through a series of Instagram posts and videos, audiences can follow Yunus as he navigates his new home while supporting family overseas. Followers can view Yunus' regular updates, including curated text, photos and artwork. User interaction and comments will be integrated into the final documentary.

5. Distribution, exhibition— the new platforms

For many of us more 'established' filmmakers there is nothing new in the concept of working intensively to take films to the public. Taking our 'docs' out on the road, and mounting limited theatrical screenings and events around them, was something we all did; but it was restricted by the publicity we could muster: pinning up posters on community notice boards, depositing flyers in cafes, chatting up friendly journalists to write a story, and hoping for 'word of mouth'. The TV broadcast eventually happened, after which you would put the film into the hands of an educational distributor, then step away and get on with the next project. Now, with the help of the internet and social media platforms, filmmakers are able to carry their documentaries much further than they could ever have done before. They don't need a distributor. They can self-distribute using cinema-on-demand platforms, YouTube, Facebook and many more new and yet to be invented.

All these platforms, especially cinema-on-demand, are labour intensive. The team at Demand.Film or Fanforce will help sort out the cinema, create your Facebook event page for online ticket sales, and handle the logistics. The rest is up to you, the filmmaker, and the extent of your personal and social media networks. Having a community of interest certainly helps. In the end, if not enough tickets are sold to cover the cinema hire, the screening does not go ahead.

Producers Rebecca Barry and Madeleine Hetherton of Media Stockade are very experienced working with this new platform. Films they have produced—*I Am a Girl, Call me Dad, The Opposition*—succeeded in attracting strong audiences to cinemas all over Australia. According to Hetherton, the advantages of this model of exhibition outweigh what a traditional distributor does. 'It's all about building up an audience database. With cinema-on-demand, you have access to the back end, you can email them about screenings, encourage them to bring their friends [...] It requires a filmmaker to be very active, very involved'.[36]

The popularity of cinema-on-demand as a new distribution platform has, unfortunately, yet to translate into a mechanism triggering the 40 per cent Offset at the Provisional Certificate stage, which is administered by Screen Australia. According to the Screen Australia guidelines, the trigger is the 'intention to release' in cinemas. This is usually backed up by a Letter of Intent and a distribution guarantee from a regular distributor. However, if cinema-on-demand fulfills these requirements as a distributor, why then is this not deemed acceptable by the Offset office? This doesn't seem fair, given that this new tried and tested platform is often more successful in packing people into the cinema than a regular distributor. Filmmakers are sometimes forced into deals with traditional distributors who go on to sub-licence their films with cinema-on-demand platforms anyway. Without a Provisional Certificate, small companies are often forced to go into debt to cashflow their production all the way to completion.

The dust is still settling around the new platforms. The new 'alternative content cinema' *Backtrack Boys* deployed has been relatively successful, but it could have been more so. After the first week on 44 screens the film had made a respectable $35,000. Despite this, 21 cinemas wanted to pull the film. The producer and distributor had to work very hard to restore 13 of those screens. Sometimes it can prove an advantage to start small, opening in a limited number of cinemas, then gradually building from week to week. The lesson is that today, each film needs its own distribution strategy. My overriding belief is that Australians want to see our own diverse stories writ large on screen. The distributors are behind them, but the lack of exhibition support for Australian local theatrical documentaries still needs addressing. According to Anna Broinowski:

> *The speed with which crowd-pleasing, uniquely Australian stories are bumped for US and UK imports in the multiplexes, despite local audiences clamouring to see them, is shocking. How do we build an audience for Australian films if punters can't physically see them?*[37]

Viewing habits for streaming and/or download are not yet clear. This presents a major challenge for distributors wanting to build a successful business model. Jeni McMahon and David Batty, the producers of *Black As*, had a traditional documentary background. Series One of *Black As* had a huge number of views on Facebook—over ten million on their own page—but none of this was monetised. So they focused on driving the audience to iview, and then, after an initial hold-back period, they drove the audience to VHX where people could purchase the series via download or buy a DVD set. But the conversion rate of people watching content for free and then going to purchase was very small. So at the same time they built up their YouTube channel where they had 25,000 followers. The producers have now launched the series on Facebook Watch, and, on a basis of 140,000 likes, they have been invited to monetise individual views.

> *It was and still is a slow burn, gradually building up but only after an enormous investment in time and resources. My point would be that it's not a successful model unless you can regularly release content on either platform that generates views in the many hundreds of thousands, if not millions per post.*[38]

Series of short films like *Black As* might be perfect for YouTube and Facebook, but is not a solution for feature documentary. Subscription streaming services are one alternative. In Australia there's DocPlay and BeamaFilm, and they generally provide only small returns to filmmakers. The exception is Kanopy, which has a monopoly on educational streaming. The university market remains the core of their business model—and it is a strong and growing market.

DVD is still remarkably resilient, according to distributors like Ronin Film's Andrew Pike. Pike noticed that DVD sales plummeted once the streaming services started, but have now stabilised to a low but respectable figure. 'In the education market, particularly, there are end users, mainly libraries, whether they're in an institutional or public library, that still value the hard copy on the shelf.'[39]

For Ronin, vimeo-on-demand (VoD) is growing slowly and steadily. Distributors normally have one price for the general public and another for schools, universities, TAFEs, public libraries and community groups. When the VoD platform was launched, Ronin began with extremely low streaming prices, and then increased prices threefold. The take-up remained the same and they concluded that the pay-wall was a deterrent, irrespective of the level. But is there any option for distributors? Irrespective of the platform, having good marketing materials, study guides and strong images makes all the difference, according to Pike.

Developing audiences and skillsets

With traditional audiences disappearing, filmmakers need to find ways to develop core audiences that will return again and again to documentary on whatever devices and platforms they might choose. Databases developed through cinema-on-demand that can be built and shared, is one way, YouTube channels are another. There have been so many very good documentaries made in this country (including the titles referred to in this paper) that are not accessible anywhere and never see the light of day. It should be possible to go to a YouTube channel and watch them either at no cost or through a pay-per-view window. Perhaps the National Film and Sound Archive could play a role here. They already have YouTube channels where the public has access to curated works from their collection.

Film festivals are also important in presenting both new work and in developing audience appreciation for the form. Both the Sydney Film Festival and the Melbourne International Film Festival have expanded their documentary programs, and Antenna, an exclusively documentary festival, has been through eight editions and keeps breaking attendance records. This reflects the trend internationally where film festival audiences for documentaries are surging.

As documentary practitioners we too need increasingly to be aware of the rapidly changing landscape of the industry we work in, to come together to foster the craft of documentary, and to critically engage with each other's work. To this end the Australian Documentary

Forum (OzDox) based in Sydney, arranges a series of monthly events, most of which are also available for podcast through the OzDoxForum YouTube channel.[40] Meanwhile, the annual Australian International Documentary Conference (AIDC) brings together filmmakers, corporates, broadcasters and decision makers from around the world for their four-day event, which also incorporates craft sessions and a small screening program.

6. The challenges ahead

In this Platform Paper I've contended that the Documentary project has survived and expanded beyond traditional television into many forms, and many platforms. These have included film festivals, cinema-on-demand, event screenings, streaming through subscription and on-demand. At the same time, the old broadcast sector still manages to survive, proving that new platforms do not necessarily kill off what's tried and true. But with audiences fragmenting, a number of challenges and opportunities face the sector.

It is often the case that 'factual' is conflated with 'documentary'. Documentary is not television (i.e. factual); documentary has its own character and imperatives. Sure, some can be made quickly, especially if the subject matter is contained. Historically, however, documentaries have had long gestation periods; they grow organically, are strongly authored, often question the status quo; and the story often develops in unpredictable ways. A decade ago the opportunity existed to grow and develop a nation-wide cottage industry to make precisely these kinds of films. Instead Screen Australia's Producer Enterprise Program, with some few exceptions, facilitated the growth of large, vertically integrated companies, which now work across different genres: drama, format television, and documentary. Most are now local branches of international companies, and are no longer Australian-owned. Surely this was not what Screen Australia's senior bureaucrats had in mind.

The auteur independents, and the small companies specialising in one-offs, struggle to survive. But it's at this cottage industry end that ambition and innovation are bred—and this is where the art of documentary is thriving. The relatively low price of cameras and editing systems has meant that many of us have by necessity become multi-skilled, and go some way towards making our next documentary, before starting the increasingly fraught process of applying for funding. In some cases colleagues have shot and edited their films themselves, and receive agency support only at the end (through the PEP scheme). This process can often take years and be incredibly frustrating. But recent examples prove these films do brilliantly well. Obviously the business plan requires some personal savings, or juggling between production work on other people's films and one's own. It also helps to have a good editor on board to give shape to a documentary often carved from two hundred plus hours of rushes. The editor is the director's key collaborator, and in Australia we have editors of world class.

But these opportunities require financial resources which are not available to filmmakers at the start of their careers. Usually, with the benefit of tertiary studies, and having completed one or two short documentaries, they strike out on their own. There's a limited market for one-hour films, so they set out on making a feature straightaway. However great the technical skills they might have developed on affordable cameras, this is a big 'ask'. The ones that survive in a very crowded marketplace must not only have a good idea, but be very resourceful *and* competent storytellers.

The legendary American documentary film producer, Diane Weyermann, who was behind a number of high profile and Oscar-winning documentaries, including *Citizenfour* and *Inconvenient Truth,* is one who believes that passion and commitment are the fuel that drives documentary filmmakers.

The documentary world is not driven by money or the business but driven by a person's commitment to a story and how doggedly they pursue it, financing or not.[41]

As Weyermann implies, there is a whole new generation of filmmakers around the world who don't rely on grants. They are unstoppable! But how can we then create a viable industry—a sustainable industry where filmmakers *can* cultivate their passion *and*, heaven help us, earn a living wage? The role of nurturing has traditionally fallen to the agencies. Screen Australia has been especially proactive—but they could do more, as could the state agencies, which appear simply to follow what the federal agency is doing. This is, after all, the critical area where early career filmmakers get their break and develop their craft.

In its most recent Corporate Plan, Screen Australia re-states its 'vision and purpose' as being 'to encourage quality, innovation and cultural value through programs that increase the ambitions, risk tolerance and diversity of Australian storytelling.'[42] In the spirit of these objectives, the agency needs to comprehensively review its funding programs in consultation with the industry. Screen Australia must allocate a greater percentage of its resources towards documentary, both in the development area, and especially to the Producer Program, on which the calls to support more features are ever increasing. I have referred to the box office and critical success that documentary features have had in the crowded exhibition sector. I believe Screen Australia must take stock of this and reward the sector by funding it at a more generous level. The agency should also re-focus its Enterprise Program in order to buttress the viability of smaller companies. This occurred on a small scale in 2015–16 and 2016–17, but has since ceased.

One area where Screen Australia has been very pro-active is the Gender Matters initiative in Australia.[43] Once there were primarily men making documentaries. The latest statistics now show that 49 per cent of documentary producers and 38 per cent of directors are women. State agencies have started to play an important role here, as well as in encouraging production in non-metropolitan areas and from culturally and linguistically diverse communities. But there is still room for improvement.

We are now at another historical moment—one of transition from a rapidly outdated broadcast model to a digital future made up of many platforms. But this new paradigm cannot survive without some sort of government regulation underpinning it. The expanding delivery systems created by the internet will be the future. Netflix, Amazon Prime, and Stan are making millions of dollars from streaming mainly North American and British-made content onto our various devices. Netflix is now accessed by 9.8 million Australians, according to Roy Morgan data published in August—up 30 per cent from the year earlier. Yet Netflix only offers 1.5 per cent of Australian content, according to RMIT research.[44] Sure, Netflix has made a few acquisitions such as Susan Lambert and Stefan Moore's *Tyke Elephant Outlaw*, Jeff Daniels' *Mother with a Gun* and Anna Broinowski's *Aim High in Creation*. But these have been isolated purchases. Currently they have no local content obligations. These companies must be forced to get involved in Australian-originated documentary projects right from the start.

I see no reason why these digital service providers and streaming services should not be governed by the same kind of content regulations as the commercial broadcasters. Quotas have been enforced previously on commercial free-to-air networks, so the precedents have been set. It's not going to happen any other way. In September 2017, the government of Canada struck a deal with Netflix that committed the company to invest $400 million in Canadian productions over five years.

Meanwhile the European Parliament approved a set of guidelines by which a minimum of 30 per cent of all content carried on streaming services operating in the European Union will have to come from the region. Surely it's inevitable that the same thing will happen here—that Netflix and Amazon Prime will come within a regulatory environment to commission Australian content. These streaming services could potentially become key players in commissioning Australian documentaries, as has happened in the US. This is why quotas are not just necessary, they are essential.[45]

As we go down the path of regulation we should keep in mind the ubiquitous nature of documentary: that niche projects have equal intrinsic value to 'blockbuster' documentaries. We owe it to our predecessors to preserve the rich diversity of the form that historically has given us so many memorable works. Independent documentary filmmakers are the chroniclers of our age, the narrators of our nation. It is vital that we keep making documentaries and preserve them for our children and their children. It will be these films that will tell the true stories of our time.

Endnotes

1   Martha Ansara, *The Shadowcatchers: A History of Cinematography in Australia*. Sydney: Australian Cinematographers Society, 2008.

2   Hugh McInnes quoted in *The Shadowcatchers*.

3   A detailed account of the Realist Film Unit and their body of films can be found in John Hughes, *The Archive Project: The Realist Film Unit in Cold War Australia*. ATOM Inc. 2013; and a feature documentary of the same name (2006).

4   Martha Ansara and Lisa Milner. 'The Waterside Workers Federation Film Unit: the Forgotten Frontier of the Fifties', *Metro Magazine* no. 119, 1999: pp.28–39.

5   Ross Lansell and Peter Beilby (eds), 'The Documentary Film in Australia', in *Cinema Papers* in association with Film Victoria, 1982.

6   John Hughes, 'A Work in Progress: the Rise and Fall of Australian Filmmakers Co-operatives, 1966–86', *Senses of Cinema* Issue 77, 2015.

7   John Hughes, 'After Indonesia Calling', exegesis submitted to RMIT University, Melbourne, November 2012, p.131.

8   Trish FitzSimons, Pat Laughren, Dugald Williamson. *Australian Documentary: History, Practices and Genres*.Port Melbourne, Vic.: Cambridge University Press, 2011 p.85.

9   Sharon Bell and Lisa Noonan, 'An Overview Paper of Australian Documentary Production, prepared for the Second Australian Documentary Conference, November 1991, p.12.

10   Australian Screen Directors Association, minutes of Documentary Sub-Committee, 25 March 1996.

11   Film Australia 2006 Annual Report, pp.36–37.

12   John Hughes, 'Ten Conditions of Documentary,' *Arena Magazine* 110, February 2011.

13   Documentary Production and Funding in Australia, AFC discussion paper, 2004.

14   Document presented by Michael Cordell to a group representing Sydney-based documentary filmmakers held at FFC offices, May 2007.

15   FitzSimons, Laughren, Williamson, p.158.

16   There was a robust interchange of views about the future of Film Australia in an email discussion forum, called the Australian Documentary Filmmakers Policy Forum, which operated for almost a decade. Ansara's and O'Rourke's comments were posted in July 2007.

17   Session on documentary funding recorded at the AIDC Conference held in Adelaide, March 2011.

18   Trevor Graham, quoted in *The Australian*, 6 September 2012.

19   Sharon Connolly, 'Strewth—Everything you always wanted to know about the one-off documentary but were too afraid to ask'. Report commissioned by AFTRS July 2013.

20   Kim Dalton, *Missing in Action: The ABC and Australia's screen culture*, Platform Paper 51, May 2017.

21   Interview with Dr Mitzi Goldman, CEO, Documentary Australia Foundation via GOOD PITCH[2] Australia 2016.

22   Interview with Teri Calder, recorded 14 November 2018.

23   Screen Australia's allocation for documentary started at $15.6 million in 2012/13, briefly went up to $19 million in 2014/15, and has now in 2017/18 settled back to $15.59 million.

24   Steve Bibb, email to the author, 7 December 2018.

25   'Regarding BBC Studios, Foreign Formats and Production Company Fees', collective letter on behalf of 37 producers to Screen Australia. 25 May 2018.

26   Regarding BBC Studios.

27   Michael Brealey, Reported in *Screenhub* 22 Aug 2018.

28   Reported in *Variety*, 9 November 2018.

29   The Producer Program is designed 'to support innovative documentaries with a strong creative vision', [...] projects will need to demonstrate a highly developed understanding of how they reach and engage their target market and audience.'

30   Sam Griffin, 'Introducing the Progressive Model for Feature Documentaries', thesis submitted to Master of Screen Arts and Business, AFTRS, June 2017. Executive summary, p.1.

31   Sam Griffin.

32   PEP is a direct payment of funds to producers of eligible Australian documentaries, equal to 20 per cent of the approved budget. It's been a popular program because

filmmakers are free to make their documentary using their own funds in the knowledge that they can finish them, as long as they provide proof of future distribution or an end user. In 2017–18 PEP provided $3.36 million to 54 titles.

33   Interview with Anna Broinowski, recorded 13 November 2018.

34   Margie Bryant, interview with the author, 20 November 2018.

35   Ivan O'Mahoney, by email, 9 November 2018.

36   Madaleine Hetherton, interview recorded 20 November 2018.

37   Anna Broinowski, interview 13 November 2018.

38   Interview with Jeni McMahon, 12 November 2018.

39   Interview with Andrew Pike, recorded 20 October 2018.

40   OzDox podcast list: http://www.ozdox.org/podcasts/

41   Reported in *Variety*, 9 November 2018.

42   Screen Australia Corporate Plan 2018–19, p.2.

43   Gender Matters is a suite of initiatives by Screen Australia started in 2016 aimed at addressing the gender imbalance within the Australian screen industry.

44   'Australian content in SVOD catalogs' by Ramon Loato and Alexa Scarlata, RMIT.

45   The Screen Producers Association has estimated that a quota of ten per cent on Stan, Netflix, Telstra and Fetch would yield $100 million for the industry annually.

COPYRIGHT INFORMATION

PLATFORM PAPERS
Quarterly essays from Currency House Inc.
Founding Editor: Dr John Golder
Editor: Katharine Brisbane
Currency House Inc. is a non-profit association and resource centre advocating the role of the performing arts in public life by research, debate and publication.

Postal address: PO Box 2270, Strawberry Hills, NSW 2012, Australia
Email: info@currencyhouse.org.au Tel: (02) 9319 4953
Website: www.currencyhouse.org.au Fax: (02) 9319 3649

ISBN 978-0-6484265-1-6
ISSN 1449-583X

Typeset in Garamond
Printed by Ligare Book Printers, Riverwood, NSW
Production by Currency Press Pty Ltd

FORCHCOMING

PP No.59, May 2019

AUSTRALIAN INDIGENOUS MUSIC TODAY

Christopher Sainsbury

This paper explores a range of contemporary Indigenous music styles from country to rap, and from rock to classical. The artists are selected to show the diversity of their age and background, country, language, and circumstance. Through these musicians the author examines aspects of Australian Indigenous experience of identity, community, relationship to land, expression of culture, Australian history and the demands of the music industry. Many of our leading musicians do not live in their community, he emphasises, but where the music industry thrives—in our cities. It's practical and often results in fruitful collaborations that are good business, but also encourage traditional cultural practice: practical and ceremonial exchange between clans. The study outlines and clarifies aspects of a growing and dynamic cultural biography brought into the music industry from our First Peoples' older traditions, and the recurring political and social issues of all Australians.

Christopher Sainsbury is an internationally recognised Indigenous composer and teacher. His working method in this paper is a mix of musical analysis, participant observation, ethnography and personal experience.

AT YOUR LOCAL BOOKSHOP FROM 1 MAY

AND AS A PAPERBACK OR ONLINE

FROM OUR WEBSITE AT

WWW.CURRENCYHOUSE.ORG.AU